THE LITTLE BOOK
of LIGHT

*One Hundred Eleven Ways
to Bring Light into Your Life*

Mikaela Katherine Jones

Conari Press

First published in 2012 by Conari Press, an imprint of
Red Wheel/Weiser, LLC
With offices at:
665 Third Street, Suite 400
San Francisco, CA 94107
www.redwheelweiser.com

ISBN: 978-1-57324-577-7

Library of Congress Cataloging-in-Publication Data is available
on request.

Cover design by Jim Warner
Cover illustration: Dave Stevenson
Interior by Maureen Forys, Happenstance Type-O-Rama
Typeset in Historical Fell

Printed in China
GWP

10 9 8 7 6 5 4 3 2

The paper used in this publication meets the minimum require-
ments of the American National Standard for Information
Sciences—Permanence of Paper for Printed Library Materials
Z39.48-1992 (R1997).

This book is dedicated to my mom, who carried me through my childhood with her light, a light more brilliant than the sun, and who ushered me into adulthood with the awareness that the light I saw in her was a reflection of the light in me.

Darkness cannot drive out darkness;
only light can do that.
Hate cannot drive out hate;
only love can do that.
—MARTIN LUTHER KING, JR.

Angels can fly because they take themselves
lightly.
—G.K. CHESTERTON

ILLUMINATE YOUR PATH
to DELIGHT

No matter where you live, who you know,
or what has or hasn't happened to you, you
deserve to delight in life . . . daily. You are
here to make manifest your True Self, share
your unique gifts . . . and shine. These are in
fact your divine birthrights.

But we all know it's not easy. Sometimes
the path can appear dark and treacherous.
Perhaps you're working through overcoming
a childhood trauma or grieving over the loss
of a close loved one. (I've been there.) Or perhaps you just got a scary medical diagnosis,
or had your heart broken. (I've been there,
too.) Or maybe you're just having a bad day
and need some extra light to stay steadfast
on your path? (We've all been there.)

When it comes down to it, life is a series of experiences, which are comprised of a series of moments. And in each moment, we have a choice. We can choose to perceive from our True Self—a state of expanded awareness that is the source of our highest potential, and is characterized by feelings of love, peace, empowerment, and joy—*or* we can choose to react from the darkness of our wounded, limited self, which is characterized by feelings of unworthiness, separation, sadness, and fear.

When you remember that everyone on the planet is a brave spiritual being here on a wild, physical adventure, and therefore deserves compassion (especially you), your ability to respond to the moment in positive and powerful ways grows exponentially. As you practice seeing and responding to life from the awareness of your True Self, your heart opens . . . and you begin to feel the love and delight that are ever-present to you. The more you practice living from your True Self, the more life brings you experiences of peace, appreciation, and love. And as you continue to practice, you will be better able to *choose* peace, love, and appreciation amidst the darker times as well.

It is my deepest prayer that *The Little Book of Light* will help illuminate your path, and gently guide you out of the darkness so that you can make manifest your True Self. May it help you find delight daily, so you will have the energy reservoir you need to stay on path toward the fulfillment of your personal vision.

This book is not just "light" reading. I know from my own personal experience (and from sharing the Ways with clients), that practicing these 111 Ways will help you live your most important, fulfilled life ... with delight ... daily. When you practice with an open heart and mind, your life will shine. And you, in your own special way, will become a lighthouse of peace, love, and delight.

HOW TO READ
THE LITTLE BOOK OF LIGHT

Dear Reader,

Let me count the ways you can read from *The Little Book of Light*. You can read it straight through, perhaps in your favorite chair, or in a hammock under a grand tree, or on the beach with your toes in the warm sand.

The ability to find delight takes practice, so I recommend regarding *The Little Book of Light* as your devoted spiritual confidante or cheerleader. Keep it somewhere close, like on your nightstand or your work desk, in your purse or your car's glove compartment, and simply ask God/Divine Mind/Source/ Infinite Spirit (or however you choose to call your higher power): "How can I bring more light into my life? How can I manifest my True Self and fulfill the personal vision I hold for my life?" Then randomly open the book and see what your answer is. Or, you can meditate on a different Way each day, and when you get to the end of the book, simply start over.

The 111 Ways in *The Little Book of Light* will help you with different aspects of your life. Some will help you perceive your life from the perspective of your expanded consciousness, your True Self, so that you may face life's inevitable challenges with more strength, grace, and ease. Some will help you interact with others and the world with more harmony, sweetness, and intimacy. And still others will help you get in touch with the gifts of your inner child, enabling you to more deeply experience the magic and beauty of the present moment so that you can truly delight in life.

With Love and Delight,
♥ —MIKAELA

111 Ways *to* Bring Light *into* Your Life

1.

Listen to that calm, peaceful
voice inside . . . It's the voice of your heart,
which always has the most illumination
in any situation.

2.

Release your attachment to
your intended outcomes.
While it is paramount to *set intentions*,
it is best to then turn them over to God . . .
because God may have a different
and *better* plan for you.

3.

You are a gift to the world
with your very BEING.
Nobody has your unique energy, smile, or laugh.
Without you, life's rich human rainbow
wouldn't be complete.

4.

Hum.
Proud and out loud, or softly to yourself.
The vibration of humming calms and soothes you,
and helps you feel your innate peace and love.
This is really fun to do in store lines
or in the doctor's office.
Hum softly and brighten the room
with your love.

5.

Close your eyes and visualize yourself
as a glorious, radiant sun.
Picture the center of your sun shining forth
from your heart or your belly.
Feel the sun's warmth melt away any tension
or tightness in your body.
Feel the love and the power that naturally
emanate from you.

6.

Be conscious of things
that make you smile.
Like children's laughter.
It is from the place of feeling good
and feeling gratitude that
we are able to bring our dreams
into reality . . .
So let the good times
and the tears of gratitude roll.

7.

Speak from your center.
Observe your breath.
If it's quick and shallow, you're probably
not centered. Take a few deep breaths and
set the intention to speak from your heart
so you can say what you really mean.

8.

Let the power and tenderness of your heart
heal your should-haves,
your could-haves,
and your wish-I-would-haves.

9.

Count your blessings.
Our lives are bursting with them.
There is always something
for which to be grateful.
Always.
It is through a consistent attitude of gratitude
that we create a magical
and delight-filled life.

10.

Watch the sunset.
Watch flowers watch the sunset!
I was out walking one evening and noticed
a bougainvillea tree full of magenta flowers
bending to the sun as it set.
They shimmered in the breeze as if they
were clapping at the performance.
A delightful sight.

11.

Be true to yourself.
If you ignore your heart's desires
and are only true to others,
you exhaust yourself.
Being true to yourself while being
kind and compassionate with others
energizes the soul.

12.

Your perception reigns supreme.
If your perception of something is making
you feel bad, try on a new perception.
We always have the freedom to choose
how we look at something.
For example, "I lost my job; I'm worthless,"
can become
"I wonder what wonderful opportunity
is going to open up for me now
to do what I truly love, utilizing some of the skills
I have gained in this last job?"

13.

Stroke a dog's head. Play with your kitty.
Or cuddle your hamster
or your rabbit or your mouse.
If you don't have one,
just visualize and pretend.
It will have the same uplifting effect
on your energy.

14.

Toss worry out the window.
Instead of focusing on what you
don't want to happen, focus on what
you *do* want to happen. You *always*
have the opportunity to create an
avenue to delight, no matter where
you are now.
Hold the end goal as your vision . . .
FEEL IT,
and let your heart guide you . . .
step by step.

15.

Believe in angels.
If you believe, you will feel their presence often.
Ask them for guidance, comfort, and love.
They are honored to be of service,
but you must ask first.
Ask, ask, ask . . .
and then ask some more.

16.

Close your eyes and just breathe.
First breathe deep into your belly,
then chest,
and then upper back.
Visualize inhaling peace and love . . .
and exhaling any tension or worry.
You can picture a golden or pink light
on the inhale . . .
and as you exhale, picture smoke or
dust being released.
Do at least ten rounds of these deep,
conscious breaths each day.

17.

Become aware of your self-talk.
If you find yourself saying,
"I'm so sad . . ."
or "I'm so depressed,"
catch it, and say,
"Well, that's a depressing thought.
I know this too shall pass."
This slight difference in the way you speak
to yourself will shift your energy
and make you
feel lighter.

18.

When the rollercoaster of life
gets bumpy, take a break and give gratitude
for how far you've come.
Find something in your surroundings
or in your accomplishments to appreciate.
Breathe . . .

19.

Practice positive speaking.
Try eliminating all gossip and complaints
for just today . . . Gossip and complaining
only bring your energy down and make
you feel worse. Try it for today . . .
and you might joyfully commit for life.

20.

Hold your head high.
You are a radiant, beautiful,
and powerful being of light.

21.

Choose to focus on the positive in others.
Set your intention in the morning . . .
"Today I choose to see the good in
everyone . . . Through the shadows
and clouds of their illusion,
I will affirm their light."
The more you practice this,
the more delight life will bring you.

22.

Get grounded.
Commune with nature.
Go barefoot.
Listen to the birds.
Watch the sun dance
through the leaves of the trees.
Smell the earth.

23.

Create your life according to your own values.
You will have a much more fulfilling life.
Release the need for approval from others.
You were not put here to live your father's life
or your grandmother's or your sister's . . .
you were put here to make your contribution
to the world in your own unique and delightful way.

24.

Become conscious of the choices you make
moment by moment.
Life is not a series of things . . .
life is a series of experiences,
which is a series of moments.
How you experience and choose
to react to something
is solely up to you.
Choose with awareness.

25.

Sing to someone or
something you love.
It makes no difference if
it's your friend,
or your fish,
or your ficus.

26.

Stretch—your body *and* your mind.
An open mind that seeks understanding
rather than jumping to judgment
is a conduit of light and love.

27.

Honor yourself by having a personal vision.
Visualize an acorn or a sunflower seed
in the palm of your hand . . .
notice how small they are . . .
and now
visualize the mighty oak tree that
the acorn will become . . .
and the proud, beautiful sunflower the tiny seed
will grow into . . .
That same potential for growth and beauty
lives in you . . .
what will you one day become?

28.

Music has the power to shift your energy quickly.
So listen to music that makes you feel *good*.
If you feel angry or anxious,
dancing to "raucous" music can help move
the negative energy out of your body.
Or, if you need a good cry,
play a moving piece of classical music.
Make sure you follow up
with music that makes you feel
calm and uplifted.

29.

Celebrate yourself!
Don't limit your radiant self-expression.
You encourage others to
shine bright
through your own example.
And don't let those naysayers get you down.
Share your joy only with those
whom you know will celebrate with you.
You can always share your joy with God
by being grateful.
In-Joy!

30.

Imagine standing under a waterfall
of brilliant light. Inhale the light
into your body, and notice the
dance of rainbows within the sparkling light.
Let it flow through the top of your head,
down through your shoulders and back,
into each and every muscle
and cell of your body.
Thank it for relaxing, healing,
and rejuvenating your entire body.

31.

Love your body.
Feed it nourishing foods . . .
get it moving . . .
give it rest.
Speak to it with
gratitude, not condemnation.
Your body is your Temple . . .
your Temple of light and
delight . . .
if you will only treat it as such.

32.

Say yes to life!
Own your gifts. Give it your all.
"Give me an 'L'! Give me an 'I'!
Give me a 'V'! Give me an 'E'!
L–I–V–E, LIVE!"

33.

Visualize what you'd like to create
in your life. Be specific.
What you focus on grows.
Imagine you are experiencing it now.
Feel the delicious feelings of having it.
Follow your joy and take action on the most
exciting thing you can do at this moment.

34.

Slow down.
Allow yourself to be delighted
by the simple things in life—
The feel of a cool breeze
on a hot summer day.
The ant determinedly carrying
its family's food on its back.
The two small white butterflies dancing
among the magenta bougainvillea
outside the window as I write this.
What a treat!

35.

Remember: You are free to
use your imagination in creative ways
to create more moments of delight.
For example, when I'm sitting in traffic,
I picture the cars as fish and the SUVs and
trucks as sea turtles. I say or think to myself,
"We all move in harmony . . . arriving at our
destinations with ease and grace."
The traffic always lightens!

36.

Whenever you feel afraid,
call on God and your angels to be with
you . . . Ask them to protect you and
surround you with an impenetrable
shield of light and love.

37.

Become acquainted with a flower.
Get right up close and take it in.
Imagine what it is like to *be* the flower.
If you have an open mind and heart,
a rush of delight will
wash over you as you do this.
Flowers are powerhouses of light.

38.

Practice seeing the world with
the eyes of your inner child.
Expand your capacity to
experience awe
and wonder.
When we use the eyes
of our inner child, the world
becomes a magical playground
of delight and synchronicity.

39.

Shake it out.
Whenever you feel nervous or anxious,
shake out your arms and legs.
Gently bounce on the soles of your feet.
Move the energy out of your body.
Take a few deep breaths,
and feel yourself returned to your center.

40.

Give somebody a hug . . .
and get hugged in return.

41.

Act as if you are already the person you
dream of becoming . . .
courageous, self-expressed,
and compassionate.
When you get anxious, ask yourself,
"How would the 'I'
whom I want to become
act in this situation?"
Then do it . . .
You'll be amazed how much
you already are the you *you* desire to be.

42.

Send the whole world light.
Imagine holding the earth in the palm of
your hands, surrounding it with brilliant,
golden light. Visualize the light infusing the
entire planet and every being upon it with
peace, love, and well-being.

43.

Take your dog for a walk.
If you don't have a dog,
take yourself for a walk.
It will clear your head,
quiet your ego,
and make room for
more light.

44.

Follow your Divine Inspiration.
Trust in your intuition's
sometimes winding path.
Seize the day!
Be courageous; act on it.

45.

Let go of the past.
Cut the shackles and live today
as if it were the first day
of the rest of your life . . .
It is.

46.

Make it a priority to ENJOY yourself today . . .
Make a list of at least three things you will do
today that will leave you tickled pink.
They don't need to be expensive
or time-consuming.
Smell a flower. Look at yourself in the mirror
and make a silly face, or tell yourself, "I love you."
Also, remember to tell others how much
you love them.

47.

See people's differences and eccentricities
as treasures of humanity.
We are *all* oddballs in one way
or another. Judgment and harsh words
don't serve anybody;
they only throw a cloud
over your own light.

48.

Give up your need to be perfect.
As long as you're in your body,
you still have things to learn and
experience. It is not your job to be
perfect; it is your job to share
your unique gifts and your love.
In so doing, you will inspire
and uplift others.

49.

Sing without caring if others can hear.
Oh, it's so much fun.
Okay, close your windows if you must . . .
Then belt it!

50.

Be a tribute to unconditional love.
It is not our role to judge others . . .
Ours is only to be a stand
for love, compassion, and light.

51.

Try this if you're ever in a dark place . . .
or when you're not!
Close your eyes and imagine someone
you love smiling at you.
When you physically feel yourself begin to smile,
send them a blessing of love and gratitude.

52.

Try on compassion when you feel least able.
That guy cutting you off in traffic—
Do you know for sure he's not rushing to get
to the hospital before his baby is born?
Or to catch his loved one before they die?
He probably needs your blessings.

53.

Choose to be courageous.
Your mind can only focus on one thing at a
time, so when you choose to be courageous,
you focus on your strength and power
and magically overcome your fear.
The beauty is that no matter the outcome,
you will feel lighter for having
shown such courage.

54.

Practice sharing.
Find a charity that inspires you . . .
Share your time, your money,
and your love.
Share your complaints
and your fears with God only,
and watch your delight grow
exponentially.

55.

Laugh at yourself.
You're very funny.
Come on . . . you're hysterical!
You know you are.

56.

Trust in the process of your life.
Even if something "bad" happens.
Have faith that something *good*
will come out of it . . .
It may take awhile to see the blessing,
but eventually you will.

57.

Believe in yourself and your dreams.
You are a radiant being of light and love.
You are deserving of your dreams
just the way you are.

58.

Close your eyes and turn your face to the sun.
Breathe in the light . . .
Or imagine you are lying on the warm sand
of a tropical beach,
your face turned to the sun.
With practice, this will have the same effect
on cloudy days
as it does on sunny days . . .

59.

The only way to win big in life is if
you're willing to make big mistakes,
and look ridiculous.
We often take life so seriously,
even though we're all going to
end up the same way—free
from our bodies and one with our light.
So what have you got to lose?
You might just win BIG!

60.

Practice yoga.
Stretching your body
while focusing on your breath
opens you to more positive energy.
Get your glow on!

61.

Become a steward of the earth.
Plant a tree. Recycle.
Pick up pieces of trash
others have left behind.
Use less electricity.
Thank the earth for her beauty,
her bounty, and her boundless
regenerative powers.

62.

Be with your feelings.
If you're angry, punch a pillow.
If you're sad, cry.
Be present and simply allow
the feeling to happen.
Notice that you're *having* a feeling.
The feeling isn't who you are.
By noticing it, it will transform
more quickly to a lighter feeling.
Feel and observe your feelings,
and they will be released
and transformed.

63.

Be gentle with yourself.
Falling down is a part of life.
Get back up and allow
your True Self to guide you.
Soon you'll be shining even brighter.
Most bright lights fall down many times
before they learn to fly.

64.

Practice the feeling of RELIEF
that is at your command.
Relax your body and mind.
Here's one way to practice:
Picture the outcome you want.
Imagine looking through your eyes, smiling,
and see your loved ones smiling back at you.
If you practice this often,
your worries will fade,
and you will come to attract delight . . .

65.

Practice the feeling of RELIEF
for whoever may need it . . .
for the world.
Get quiet, close your eyes, and visualize . . .
Picture the person or area or people
experiencing relief. Picture them feeling
capable and strong. See them wiping
their tears and smiling . . .
Feel *your relief* at the situation easing . . .
We are all connected . . .
so as you feel and visualize
this feeling of relief,
you positively impact the world.

66.

LIGHTEN UP.

Get rid of all the extra clutter in your home.
Lightening your load will lighten your life.

67.

Dance.
It's okay, nobody's watching.
Move as slowly or as crazily as you like.
One of my earliest memories of being aware
of my True Self was as a young child
dancing. There was nowhere else I wanted
to be and there was always the moment—
I'd watch and wait for it—
when I knew that "I" wasn't dancing,
but that God was dancing me.

68.

Give of your love freely . . .
without expectation.
The universe is always in
an exchange of energy.
When you give of your love freely,
it will inevitably be given back to you . . .
just not perhaps from where you first gave it.

69.

Detoxify your mind.
Resolve to avoid knee-jerk reactions and
judgments . . . Have compassion
for yourself and others.
You'll be amazed
at the delightful interactions
that open up for you.

70.

Embrace your inherently playful nature.
Go to the park . . . Roll in the grass . . .
Appreciate the flowers.

71.

Seek your own counsel.
Instead of asking everybody else's opinion,
ask your True Self
and trust in the answers given.
Ask yourself, "What would my True Self do?"
If you don't get a response, try:
"If I knew what my True Self would do
in this situation,
what would it be?"

72.

True spirituality is the energy of inclusivity.
All are included
in the whole as One with love.
Exclusivity resides only in the human mind,
not in the heart of God.

73.

Keep a "delightful moments" journal.
My entry for today:
The tiny rainbows in
the droplets of dew on my cat's grass on the
windowsill, the taste of a peach,
the freedom felt in singing with abandon,
the love in my friend's eyes as she gave me
an early Christmas present (in July!!),
the exhilaration of the two Indian dancers,
the wild sky driving home,
and the lightning on the bay,
which all lead to my favorite words in the world:
"Thank you, thank you, thank you God."

74.

Know your goals of *being*.
Be compassionate, creative,
and of service . . .
Watch how your material goals manifest naturally
out of organizing your life to fulfill
your goals of *being*.

75.

Accept yourself for where you are now
and do the best you can.
Take heart in knowing that
the universe rewards
not only actions that have good outcomes,
but actions taken with good intentions.

76.

Practice being present with others.
Really listen, rather than just thinking about
what you're going to say next.
People can sense
when they've been truly heard.
Being present is a *present*
to yourself and others.

77.

Give others a break.
We all make mistakes.
Try being angry for only fifteen minutes.
Make a deal with your mate or a loved one.
Fifteen minutes.
And if you can be angry for only fifteen minutes,
why not make it ten?

78.

Discover your purpose.
Many believe that before we come into this
life, we choose a purpose . . . a mission.
Do you know what yours is?
Listen to your heart,
the voice of your True Self,
and declare your purpose.

79.

Speak with authority and conviction . . .
and know when to be silent.
There is great wisdom and illumination in both.
Ask your heart which is the best approach
for that moment
and proceed with confidence.

80.

Be yourself.
You are a treasure unto the world.

81.

Treat ALL life as sacred. . . .
It is.

82.

Be generous in the giving of yourself.
Even if it's just for a moment.
You could be the person
who makes all the difference.

83.

There is no such thing as an accident.
There is only your True Self
trying to get your attention.
Ask your heart what the message is.

84.

Find the good in everything.
What we call darkness and pain
are also of vaule.
If we pay attention to their lessons,
they can help us grow and evolve.
Our light doesn't shun the darkness.
It embraces it and
transforms it into a gift.

85.

Whenever you are missing a deceased friend,
family member, or pet . . . remember back
to a time with them when you were sharing
a moment of delight and love.
Step back into that feeling, and set the intention
to send them love. They have
passed onto a higher frequency, so if you'd
like to share love with them now, you will
be far more successful when you connect
with them through the energy of your
remembered joy, rather than your sorrow.
Just try it . . . you'll be amazed by how easy and
sweet an experience this can be.

86.

Forgive your mistakes.
Live wisely in the NOW.
Making mistakes builds character,
which makes it become easier to be
compassionate with others.

87.

Be a person of your word.
To shine bright in life,
you must live with integrity.
As a person of your word, not only will your
trust in yourself *and* life grow
exponentially, but you will become
a person you and others admire.

88.

Honor the cues of your body.
When you're tired . . . rest.
Think of it as a sacred duty
rather than a luxury.

89.

Have faith.
Remember . . .
God wouldn't give you an inspiration
without the ability to make it happen.

90.

Release your expectations.
Set your intention . . .
and give gratitude in advance.
Do your best,
and be unattached to the results.
Trust in God.

91.

Appreciate your food and water.
Eat lots of raw fruits and vegetables—
organic, if you can.
Fruits and vegetables are containers of light,
nourished by light and water.
Thank your food for increasing your radiance
as it travels throughout your body.
Send a blessing to all those
who grew, handled, and prepared it.

92.

Get excited!
Have you ever seen a child tap their little feet
or jump up and down with anticipated glee?
Just imagine if you began every day
with this kind of anticipation.
Try it . . .
You'll love the way you feel and
the smile it brings to your face!

93.

Appreciate yourself.
You have already contributed so much
to life . . . just by your very being.
Your presence, your smile, and your love
has made all the difference.

94.

Be someone's anonymous angel.
Follow your heart's gentle nudge.
Recently I was shocked when a tollbooth charged
$3.75 per car.
Then I got the nudge to not only pay
the darned $3.75 for my car,
but to pay for the car behind me as well.
"But the car behind me is a Rolls,"
I said to the inner nudge.
You have no idea the ripples this could cause,
it continued.
This could inspire him to give his employees a raise,
which enables a child to go to college,
which leads to world peace.
I paid for the next two.

95.

Honor your heart.
Maintain good boundaries.
Say yes when you want to
and no when you need to.
Build trust in yourself.
Let yourself know
you've got your own back.

96.

Be kind with yourself
when you experience apparent setbacks.
They are a valuable part of life.
See them as opportunities
to reevaluate your goals and change
your course of action as needed.
Ask your inner wisdom and God
to guide you.

97.

Meditate.
Follow the flow of your breath . . .
When you allow yourself to be . . .
You shall receive . . .

98.

Become conscious of your language.
Words are power.
The *experience* of our lives
is determined by our language.
Instead of saying, "This is killing me,"
or "Oh well, that's life,"
say "This is a growth opportunity,"
or, "Something better must be coming."
Watch your words . . .
and watch your life transform.

99.

Forgive when you're ready.
Forgiveness doesn't mean you
condone what another has done to you . . .
It simply means you are freeing yourself
and moving on as someone who
survives, and even thrives in life . . .
despite the pain you suffered
as a result of another.

100.

Write down your goals.
There is magic in putting pen to paper.
Break down your goals into action steps.
What are your goals for the year?
Break it down by the month, by the week,
and then by the day.
If you follow through,
you will step out of the realm of dreamer
and into the reality of an achiever.

101.

Quantum physics shows us that at the deepest level,
we are all connected.
So by choosing to act from your heart,
you share your love with the world.
Thank you.

102.

Appreciate others.
Be generous.
Tell them of your appreciation;
don't keep it all to yourself.

103.

Pray for yourself,
for others, for the world.
Pray for those you'd rather not pray for.
Pray with presence, pray from your heart . . .
Pray like every day is a day of Thanksgiving.
It is.

104.

Remember: You are never alone.
You are always connected to your True Self.
You are always connected to the light.
Ask for deeper awareness.
Ask for guidance.
Ask to grow.

105.

Make *compassion* your word for the day . . .
your word for life . . .
your word for eternity.

106.

Give yourself love every day.
Look in the mirror and say,
"I respect you. I admire you.
I love you. . . . And by the way . . .
you're pretty cute, too."

107.

Know what is truly important to you.
There is only so much time in a day . . .
Prioritize your actions according to
the vision you hold for your life.
You deserve to be happy . . .
yet sometimes you must sacrifice
quick gratification to follow
the more fulfilling path.

108.

Reclaim your identity!
Remember that before you were a mother,
daughter, grandmother, teacher,
wife, artist, or corporate executive . . .
Before you were overweight, a recovering addict,
cancer patient, or incest survivor . . .
you were a powerful, spiritual being of light . . .
and that is who you shall be forever more.
Remind yourself of this daily . . .
hourly, if necessary . . .
and your life will transform
in powerful, positive ways.

109.

Be self-expressive.
Speak out.
Speak about what you are for
rather than what you are against.
You'll be more connected to your heart,
and more empowered.

110.

Give up your control.
You can't force anything . . .
or anyone . . . to bloom. Have faith
that a Divine Order rules your affairs . . .
There is no need to rush.

111.

Please . . . step into your True Self.
Become the bright, shining light that you truly are.
The world needs you.
All you need to do from where you are now is
take the next step . . .

Acknowledgments

First and foremost, I give my never-ending gratitude to God for consistently show-ing me how beautiful, magical, and full of delight life can be when I live consciously from my heart; from the awareness of my True Self.

I'm deeply appreciative to my mother, Pat, for awakening me to my spiritual essence at a young age. Her belief in me, my voice, and my work has made all the difference.

Special thanks go to my editor, Caroline Pincus, and my agent, Krista Goering, for clearly supporting the vision of this book. Heartfelt gratitude goes out to the whole team at Red Wheel/Weiser and Conari Press, especially Susie Pitzen, Jim Warner, and Maureen Forys!

Thank you to Monica Kibbee, Susan Bard, Victoria Andrews, and David Nicholson for all their great design and editing work on the earlier self-published versions as well.

Thanks to my beloved family, extended family, and friends—especially my beautiful sister, Christine, as well as my dear friends Casey, Cheryl, Guru Dev, Ingrid, and Jennifer, for their support, passionate minds, laughter, and love.

Big hugs to my niece, Ava, and nephews, Diego and Gabriel. May you each continue growing into the bright, shining stars you already are.

I'm also in deep appreciation for the works of Dr. John Demartini, Rev. Michael Beckwith, Gregg Braden, David Hawkins, Rick Moss, Abraham-Hicks, Les Brown, Doreen Virtue, and Landmark Education. Each affected me deeply in powerful, positive ways just when I needed it most.

Special acknowledgment goes out to my beloved helpers on the Angelic Realm. I am forever in gratitude, and I am honored to be of such sweet service.

I send a message of love on angels' wings to my father who passed away many years ago. I learned some difficult yet deeply meaningful lessons through him, and they have helped shape me into the life-loving, delight-seeking, appreciative and powerful woman I am today . . . for that I will always be grateful.

ABOUT THE AUTHOR

Mikaela Jones is an inspirational writer, speaker, Intuitive, and creator of the Delight Frequency® Manifestation Process. She has been studying consciousness and practicing hypnotherapy, meditation, and New Thought disciplines since her youth. Mikaela's work will help you stay connected with your True Self, allowing you to successfully overcome challenges and find delight daily, so you can create a fulfilled life.

To sign up for Mikaela's free Weekly Beam of Light, a short, uplifting message sent every Sunday to get your week started on the "light" track, to receive her free ten-minute audio centering meditation, or to learn more about her Delight Frequency® Manifestation Process or her Angel Readings, please visit: *www.mikaelajones.com.*

To Our Readers

Conari Press, an imprint of Red Wheel/Weiser, publishes books on topics ranging from spirituality, personal growth, and relationships to women's issues, parenting, and social issues. Our mission is to publish quality books that will make a difference in people's lives—how we feel about ourselves and how we relate to one another. We value integrity, compassion, and receptivity, both in the books we publish and in the way we do business.

Our readers are our most important resource, and we appreciate your input, suggestions, and ideas about what you would like to see published.

Visit our website, *www.redwheelweiser.com,* where you can learn about our upcoming books and free downloads, and be sure to go to *www.redwheelweiser .com/newsletter/* to sign up for newsletters and exclusive offers.

You can also contact us at *info@redwheelweiser.com.*

Conari Press
an imprint of Red Wheel/Weiser, LLC
665 Third Street, Suite 400
San Francisco, CA 94107